T0398378

Create with Me!

I LIKE TO TELL STORIES!

By Beth Gottlieb

Gareth Stevens
PUBLISHING

Please visit our website, www.garethstevens.com. For a free color catalog of all our high-quality books, call toll free 1-800-542-2595 or fax 1-877-542-2596.

Library of Congress Cataloging-in-Publication Data
Names: Gottlieb, Beth, author.
Title: I like to tell stories! / Beth Gottlieb.
Description: Buffalo, NY : Gareth Stevens Publishing, 2026. | Series: Create with me! | Includes index.
Identifiers: LCCN 2024023244 | ISBN 9781482469875 (library binding) | ISBN 9781482469868 (paperback) | ISBN 9781482469882 (ebook)
Subjects: LCSH: Storytelling–Juvenile literature.
Classification: LCC LB1042 .G68 2026 | DDC 808.5/43083–dc23/eng/20240619
LC record available at https://lccn.loc.gov/2024023244

First Edition

Published in 2026 by
Gareth Stevens Publishing
2544 Clinton St,
Buffalo, NY 14224

Copyright © 2026 Gareth Stevens Publishing

Editor: Kristen Nelson
Cover Designer: Tanya Dellaccio Keeney
Layout Designer: Nicholas Switlaski

Photo credits: Cover, p. 1 Roman Samborskyi/Shutterstock.com; pp. 5, 11, 21, 23 PeopleImages.com - Yuri A/Shutterstock.com; pp. 7, 24 (nest) junpiiiiiiiiii/Shutterstock.com; p. 9 Iren_Geo/Shutterstock.com; p. 13 Ground Picture/Shutterstock.com; p. 15, 24 (draw) Evgeny Atamanenko/Shutterstock.com; p.17 Jacob Lund/Shutterstock.com; p.19 Pixel-Shot/Shutterstock.com; p. 24 (write) Taphat Wangsereekul/Shutterstock.com.

Some of the images in this book illustrate individuals who are models. The depictions do not imply actual situations or events.

Printed in China

CPSIA compliance information: Batch #QSGS26: For further information contact Gareth Stevens, New York, New York at 1-800-542-2595.

Find us on

Contents

I like to tell stories.

I make them up!

5

I see birds building
a nest.
That would make
a good story!

I tell my toys
about a princess.
She meets a monkey!

I tell my mom a story.

It is about us.

We go to the moon!

My friend Hannah
likes stories.
She writes mine down.

13

George likes to draw.
He draws pictures
for my story!

It looks like a book!
We share it
with our class.

It is bedtime.

I tell my brother
a story.

It is about
superheroes!

It is my turn
to hear a story.
Dad tells one I like.
It is about three bears.

My imagination rests.
I can tell more
stories tomorrow!

23

Words to Know

draw

nest

write

Index